Draw Your Own Encyclopaedia

Birds

Colin M. Drysdale

Illustrated by ______________________

Pictish Beast Publications

ISBN - 978-1-909832-41-1

Published by Pictish Beast Publications, Glasgow, UK.
Published in the United Kingdom
First Printing: 2018. First Edition.

www.PictishBeastPublications.com

How To Use This Book

This is a *Draw Your Own Encyclopaedia* book for children aged six to twelve. It will provide you with interesting introductions to a variety of different areas of bird life, along with quick facts, questions you can answer and, at the end, a pop quiz where you can test the knowledge of birds which you have gained by reading this book. So far, this may seem like any other book of facts, but unlike almost every other such book, you are allowed to draw in this one. In fact, you are actively encouraged to do so! Through this, you will become the illustrator of your very own encyclopaedia chapter all about birds.

When adding your own pictures to this book, it is important that you seek out suitable images to base your own ones on. This can be done either by consulting other books, or by entering an appropriate search term into an internet search engine (such as *Google*). If you choose to use an internet search engine, the best results will usually be achieved by entering the bird's name followed by the words *Bird* and *Picture*. For example, for the first illustration on page two, the best search term to use would be *Wandering Albatross Bird Picture*. Similarly, when seeking to add additional information to pictures (such as labels for specific body parts), you will get the most useful results if you use the animal's name followed by the words *Bird* and *Labelled Diagram*. So, when you are asked to draw a labelled picture of an Archaeopteryx on page four, you will get the best results if you use the search term *Archacopteryx Bird Labelled Diagram*.

For Parents And Educators

To help ensure your child's safety online, please use appropriate online safety procedures and supervise their internet usage at all times when looking for pictures on which they can base their illustrations for this book. You can also use this time to discuss internet safety with your child, as well as strategies for searching for specific information, and how to decide whether information they find on the internet is reliable or not.

If you wish to use any of the contents of this book for educational purposes, an educational licence (which allows you to legally photocopy pages to create handouts) can be purchased from *www.pictishbeastpublications.com/draw-your-own-encyclopaedia*. Ideas for classroom activities to accompany this book can also be accessed through this webpage.

What Are Birds?

Birds are animals that have a backbone and lay eggs. They also have feathers, although in some birds, such as penguins, their feathers can look like fur. The largest living bird is the ostrich (*Struthio camelus*). It can weigh over 156 kilograms and be up to 280cm tall, but while it has feathers, just like every other bird, it cannot fly. One of the heaviest flying birds is the kori bustard (*Ardeotis kori*). It can weigh up to 18 kilograms, while the bird with the largest wingspan is the wandering albatross (*Diomedea exulans*). Its wingspan can be up to 365 centimetres, which is more than twice as long as the average adult human male is tall!

Which bird has the longest wingspan?
Write its name down and then draw a picture of it in flight here.

What is the biggest living bird?
Write its name down and then draw a picture of it here.

What is the heaviest flying bird?
Write its name down and then draw a picture of it here.

When Did Birds First Evolve?

Birds first evolved around 150 million years ago and, like mammals, they evolved from ancient reptiles. However, unlike most mammals, birds have kept a key reptilian feature – they lay eggs rather than giving birth to live young. The earliest known type of bird is called *Archaeopteryx*. We know that birds evolved from reptiles because *Archaeopteryx* had both bird-like and reptile-like features. Although it was covered in feathers, it could probably only fly for very short distances.

Quick Fact: The first fossil *Archaeopteryx* skeleton was discovered in a quarry in Langenaltheim in Germany in 1861.

Quick Fact: Liaoning Province of China is famous for its spectacular fossils of birds that lived between 110 and 130 million years ago.

What was the name of the earliest type of bird? Draw a picture of it here and label its body parts to show its bird-like and reptile-like features.

Quick Fact: *Archaeopteryx* was about fifty centimetres tall and would have weighed around one kilogram, making it about the same size as a chicken. It was probably carnivorous and most likely ate small reptiles, amphibians, mammals and insects.

Are Birds Related To Dinosaurs?

Surprising as it may seem, the answer to this is yes! Birds are the direct living descendents of a group of carnivorous dinosaurs called the Theropods, which included giant predators such as *Tyrannosaurus rex*. However, the lineage that was to eventually become the birds evolved much smaller body sizes. This small body size allowed these dinosaurs to do things that other, much larger, dinosaurs could not, including climbing trees, gliding and, eventually, flying. All other dinosaurs died out about 65 million years ago, meaning that birds are the last survivors of this once great reptile group.

Draw a picture of a theropod dinosaur and a modern bird, and then add labels to show the body parts that they have in common.

Quick Fact: Many small theropod dinosaurs had feather-like structures on their skin, meaning feathers evolved before birds.

Quick Fact: Feathers probably first evolved to keep small theropod dinosaurs warm, and were only adapted for flight later.

Can Any Birds Fly Backwards?

The wings of birds are shaped in such a way that when they are flapped, they generate lift as the air passes over them from front to back. While this allows birds to fly, it means that most birds cannot fly backwards. One group of birds, however, have evolved a very flexible shoulder joint that allows them to rotate their wings to face the other way. This means they can hover, fly sideways and even fly backwards. These are the humming birds and they are the most manoeuvrable birds on the planet!

Quick Fact: Humming birds can flap their wings at up to 200 times a second. In order to keep their flight muscles supplied with oxygen while they are doing this, their hearts need to beat at over one thousand times a minute. In contrast, a human heart will typically beat between sixty and one hundred times a minute.

What is the only type of bird that can fly backwards?
Draw a picture of one flying here.

What Is The Biggest Bird That Has Ever Lived?

The biggest bird alive today is the ostrich. Even though it can weigh over 156 kilograms and be up to 2.8 metres tall, it would be dwarfed by its distant relative, the giant moa (*Dinornis robustus*). The giant moa, found only in New Zealand, was up to 3.6 metres tall and weighed around 230 kilograms. Like the ostrich, the giant moa could not fly, but instead walked or ran everywhere on powerful legs. The giant moa, and its smaller relatives which were also endemic to New Zealand, were hunted to extinction after the islands were colonised by people about 700 years ago.

What was the name of the largest bird that has ever lived? Draw a picture of it here and draw a picture of a person standing beside it to help show how big it was.

Quick Fact: The largest flying bird ever was *Argentavis magnificens*. It was a type of vulture that lived in what is now Argentina between about nine and seven million years ago. It had a wingspan of over six metres and weighed up to seventy-two kilograms!

How Many Species Of Bird Are There?

It is hard to know exactly how many species of bird there are in the world because new species are still being discovered all the time. However, it has been estimated that there are between nine and ten thousand different bird species. The body part which varies most between different bird species is the beak, and each different shape is adapted to help the bird feed in a different way. However, some beaks can look very bizarre. For example, as its name suggest, the shoebill's beak looks like a shoe, while the spoonbill's beak looks just like a spoon!

Quick Fact: There are probably twice as many species of birds as there are of mammals, making them the most successful group of terrestrial vertebrates (animals with a backbone).

Draw the head of an eagle here, showing its hooked beak that is adapted for tearing meat.

Draw the head of a spoonbill here, showing its spoon-shaped beak that is adapted for filter-feeding .

Draw the head of a toucan here, showing its large colourful bill.

Draw the head of a pelican here, showing its massive, bucket-like beak that it uses for scooping up fish.

Draw the head of a shoebill here, showing its massive shoe-shaped beak.

Draw the head of a puffin here, showing its wedge-shaped beak that it uses to catch and hold small fish.

What Species Of Bird Lays The Largest Eggs?

Perhaps unsurprisingly, the largest eggs are laid by some of the largest birds. Of the living birds, the ostrich lays the largest eggs and the heaviest ever recorded weighed 2.6 kilograms. The extinct elephant bird laid eggs that weighed up to 10 kilograms. By comparison, a hen's egg weighs only 0.05 kilograms. However, relative to the size of the bird that lays it, the largest eggs are laid by the kiwi. Although kiwis are about the same size as a domestic chicken, their eggs are six times larger!

Quick Fact: The smallest eggs in the world are laid by the vervain hummingbird. Their eggs are only 1 cm long and weigh 0.36 g.

Quick Fact: The bird that lays the most eggs is the grey partridge. It can lay up to sixteen eggs in a single clutch!

Draw a picture of an ostrich egg, an elephant bird's egg, a hen's egg, a kiwi's egg, a vervain hummingbird's egg and a grey partridge's egg. When drawing them, make sure you label them with their name and draw them all to the same scale so that you can see how different they are in size.

What Is The Rarest Bird In The World?

Many bird species are critically endangered, meaning that there are very few of them left. This makes identifying the rarest bird in the world very difficult. However, a strong contender is the Spix's macaw (*Cyanopsitta spixii*). This bright blue parrot is native to north-eastern Brazil. Discovered in 1819, it is thought to be extinct in the wild (although one was seen in the wild in 2016). Thanks to a dedicated breeding program, there are, however, around fifty in captivity.

Quick Fact: With a population size of around 1.5 billion, the most abundant wild bird in the world is the red-billed quelea.

Quick Fact: In 1974, there were only four Mauritian kestrels left. Due to conservation efforts, there are now more than 800.

What is one of the rarest birds in the world?
Write its name down and then draw a picture of it here.

What is the most abundant wild bird in the world?
Write its name down and then draw a picture of it here.

Why Do Birds Sing?

Some of the most noticeable features of birds are the noises they make, and particularly the songs they sing. There are three main reasons why birds sing: to attract mates, to help defend their territories, and to let other birds know what species they are. In some species, bird song is accompanied by physical displays. Some of the most dramatic displays are found in the birds-of-paradise. While female birds-of-paradise are rather drab, the males are brightly coloured and many have exotic-looking feathers. In the breeding season, the males will find a tree to display in and will sing and dance, showing off their colourful plumage to attract a female with which to mate.

Can you write down three reasons why birds sing?

1.
2.
3.

Draw a picture of a male red bird-of-paradise singing and displaying to attract a mate.

Quick Fact: There are forty-two bird-of-paradise species found in New Guinea, eastern Indonesia and eastern Australia.

Quick Fact: Alex, an African grey parrot, could say over one hundred English words, and even speak in whole sentences!

What Is The World's Fastest Bird?

The fastest bird in the world is the peregrine falcon (*Falco peregrinus*). When it dives out of the sky, it can reach speeds of up to 389 kilometres per hour (or 242 miles per hour). This is faster that the fastest speed of a Formula One racing car and it makes the peregrine falcon the fastest animal in the world! However, when flying horizontally rather than diving out of the sky, it can only fly at 110 kilometres an hour (68 mph), which is about as fast as the average family car.

Quick Fact: The fastest reliably recorded speed of a bird in horizontal flight was by a gyrfalcon (*Falco rusticolus*). It is a close relative of the peregrine falcon and can reach speeds of up to 145 kilometres per hour (90 mph)!

What is the world's fastest bird?
Write its name down and then draw a picture of it here.

Which bird can reach the fastest speeds in horizontal flight?
Write its name down and then draw a picture of it here.

Can Penguins Fly?

There are seventeen species of penguin. While they are generally considered to be flightless, unlike many other flightless birds, penguins still have fully functional wings, and they can even fly! It's just that, unlike many other birds, their wings are not adapted for flying in air. Instead, they are adapted for flying through water! If you watch a penguin underwater, you will see that it moves by flapping its wings up and down, just like other birds do in the air. Although they have webbed feet, they only use these to paddle while at the surface. When underwater, their feet are only used as rudders for steering.

Draw a picture of a group of penguins flying underwater.

Quick Fact: When people think of penguins, they generally think of them swimming around icebergs in the seas of Antarctica, but not all penguins are found in cold places. The Fiordland penguin, also known as the Tawaki, nests in an area of rainforest in New Zealand while the Humboldt penguin nests in the Atacama desert in South America, and the Galapagos penguin nests close to the equator.

Pop Quiz

The answers to all these questions can be found elsewhere in this book. See if you can answer them all!

1. How many species of bird are there?
2. What was the very rare bird species you were asked to draw?
3. Can penguins fly?
4. How many birds-of-paradise species are there?
5. What is the fastest species of bird?
6. What species of bird lays the largest eggs?
7. What is the largest bird species that has ever lived?
8. What bird species lays the smallest eggs?
9. Can you name the three key characteristics of birds?
10. What is the only type of bird that can fly backwards?
11. What group of dinosaurs did birds evolve from?
12. What are the three reasons that birds sing?
13. What do pelicans use their bucket-like beaks for?
14. How big is the biggest species of living bird in the world?
15. How many Mauritian kestrels were there in 1974, and how many are there now?
16. What was the wingspan of the largest flying bird ever?

Write Your Answers Here:

1. ______
2. ______
3. ______
4. ______
5. ______
6. ______
7. ______
8. ______
9. ______
10. ______
11. ______
12. ______
13. ______
14. ______
15. ______
16. ______

Pop Quiz – The Answers

1. There are thought to be between nine and ten thousand bird species.
2. The very rare species of bird you were asked to draw in this book was the Spix's Macaw.
3. Although they are usually considered flightless, penguins can in fact fly – but only underwater!
4. There are forty-two bird-of-paradise species, all of which are found in New Guinea, eastern Australia and eastern Indonesia.
5. The fastest species of bird in the world is the peregrine falcon, which can reach speeds of up to 389 kilometres per hour (or 242 miles per hour) when diving out of the sky.
6. Of the living birds, the ostrich lays the largest eggs, but the extinct elephant bird laid eggs that were almost four times bigger than the largest ostrich egg ever recorded.
7. The largest bird species that has ever lived is the giant moa from New Zealand.
8. The smallest eggs in the world are laid by the vervain hummingbird. They are only 1 cm long and weigh 0.36 grams.
9. The three key characteristics of birds are: they have a backbone; they have feathers; and their young hatch from eggs.
10. The only type of bird that can fly backwards is the humming bird.
11. Birds evolved from a group of dinosaurs called the Theropods.
12. Birds sing to attract mates, defend their territories and to let other birds know what species they are.
13. Pelicans use their bucket-like beaks for scooping up fish.
14. The biggest living bird in the world, the ostrich, can weigh up to 156 kilograms and be up to 280 centimetres (or 2.8 metres) tall .
15. There were only four Mauritian kestrels left in 1974, but thanks to the efforts of conservationists, there are now more than eight hundred.
16. The largest flying bird ever was a type of vulture called *Argentavis magnificens*. It had a wingspan of over six metres!

Where To Find Out More About Birds

If you would like to learn more about birds, you can check out the following resources:

- **Wikipedia:** *en.wikipedia.org/wiki/Bird.*
- **Encyclopaedia Britannica:** *www.britannica.com/animal/bird-animal.*
- **The BBC:** *www.bbc.co.uk/nature/life/Bird.*
- **The RSPB:** This is an organisation dedicated to the conservation of birds in the UK and abroad. They also provide a lot of information about British birds and wildlife at *www.rspb.org.uk/birds-and-wildlife/*
- **The Illustrated Encyclopaedia of Birds:** This is an excellent book about birds and is filled with many wonderful illustrations.

Dedication

This book is dedicated to all who love animals, learning and drawing, regardless of their age!

Books available now in the *Draw Your Own Encyclopaedia* series from Pictish Beast Publications:

1. **Mammals** - ISBN: 978-1-909832-39-8. RRP: UK: £6.99 US: $8.99.
2. **Birds** - ISBN: 978-1-909832-41-1. RRP: UK: £6.99 US: $8.99.
3. **Reptiles** - ISBN: 978-1-909832-42-8. RRP: UK: £6.99 US: $8.99.
4. **Amphibians** - ISBN: 978-1-909832-43-5. RRP: UK: £6.99 US: $8.99.
5. **Fish** - ISBN: 978-1-909832-44-2. RRP: UK: £6.99 US: $8.99.
6. **Invertebrates** - ISBN: 978-1-909832-45-9. RRP: UK: £6.99 US: $8.99.
7. **Animals Box Set** – ISBN: 978-1-909832-51-0. RRP: UK: £39.99 US:$49.99.

Books coming soon in the *Draw Your Own Encyclopaedia* series:

1. **Scotland's Dolphins** - ISBN: 978-1-909832-55-8. RRP: UK: £6.99 US: $8.99.
2. **Scotland's Seabirds** - ISBN: 978-1-909832-59-6. RRP: UK: £6.99 US: $8.99.
3. **Planet Earth** - ISBN: 978-1-909832-46-6. RRP: UK: £6.99 US: $8.99.
4. **Our Solar System** - ISBN: 978-1-909832-47-3. RRP: UK: £6.99 US: $8.99.
5. **Deep Space** - ISBN: 978-1-909832-48-0. RRP: UK: £6.99 US: $8.99.
6. **The Universe** - ISBN: 978-1-909832-49-7. RRP: UK: £6.99 US: $8.99.
7. **Space Exploration** - ISBN: 978-1-909832-50-3. RRP: UK: £6.99 US: $8.99.

For more information on this series of books (including a full list of available and upcoming titles), visit: *www.pictishbeastpublications.com/draw-your-own-encyclopaedia*

Lightning Source UK Ltd.
Milton Keynes UK
UKHW04f1607270618
324868UK00005B/29/P

9 781909 832411